Planet Watch

Margaret Fetty

Rigby®
A Harcourt Achieve Imprint

www.Rigby.com
1-800-531-5015

September 2

Our teacher Mrs. Dawson said we were going to the **planetarium.** That was great news! Then she told us we would use what we learned at the planetarium to study the sky. We had to write about what we saw in an observation log. That part of the news sounded like hard work!

At the planetarium, we sat quietly in a dark room with a high, rounded ceiling. When Mrs. Dawson told us to look up, the ceiling seemed to be covered in stars. Pictures of the sun, moon, stars, planets, and other objects in the **solar system** were moving across the ceiling.

We saw how the stars look during different times of the year and how the planets travel around the sun. Mrs. Dawson told us that we could see some planets in the night sky with our very own eyes! Posters and books are nice, but it would be cool to look up at the sky and see Saturn with its rings or Mars, the red planet.

We got to see the solar system and some stars at the planetarium.

September 3

After dinner tonight I went outside to see if I could find some planets. I didn't see any planets, but I found the Big Dipper, a **constellation** that I learned about at the planetarium. It's a star pattern that looks like a measuring cup. I also saw a star that glowed more brightly than all the others. It was cool, but I was disappointed that I couldn't see any planets.

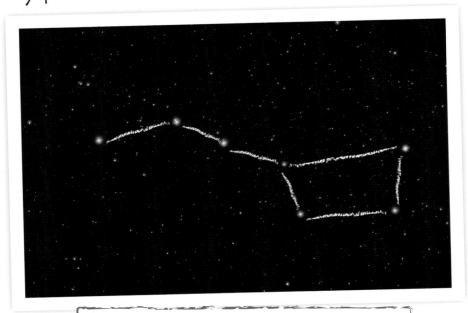

This is how the Big Dipper would look if you drew lines from star to star.

While I was looking at the sky, Grandpa came outside. He pointed at the really bright object and said, "Venus sure is bright tonight."

At first I thought he was joking. I thought that Venus would be gold, like it looks in all of the pictures. But Grandpa told me that the light from the sun shines on Venus and bounces off to make it glow like a star. I can't believe I actually saw a planet tonight after all!

Venus is to the right of the moon in this picture. It looks like a bright star.

 Check It Out!

Venus can appear at night or in the early morning. Even though it's a planet, it is called either the "evening star" or the "morning star."

This picture of Venus was taken through a powerful telescope.

September 5

I can't stop thinking about seeing Venus, and now I want to see all the other planets. Grandpa says he'll help me. He says that we have to do research so we'll know what to look for.

Now I'm excited about keeping this observation log. Way to go, Mrs. Dawson!

We found a list of things we'll need on the Internet. We're getting a sky map, which shows the positions of the stars and planets, and binoculars to see the far away planets. We'll also need a flashlight to read the sky map in the dark. Grandpa is going to help me put together our **astronomy** kit. I can't wait to get started!

things we'll need for our astronomy kit

Check It Out!

You can get sky maps. They show how the sky looks at night where you live. You get a different sky map for each month.

September 7

Tonight was the perfect night to look for planets. The moon appeared only as big as my fingernail, so the sky was really dark. Grandpa and I went outside around 7:30. Right away I saw a big, white star in the west—only I remembered that it wasn't a star. It was Venus!

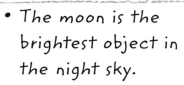

Check It Out!

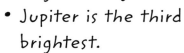

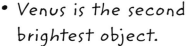

- The moon is the brightest object in the night sky.
- Venus is the second brightest object.
- Jupiter is the third brightest.

We used the flashlight to look at the sky map. The map showed that Jupiter would be close to Venus during this time of year. A little while later, I saw another white light to the right of Venus. It did not twinkle like the other stars, which was the clue I was looking for. I had found Jupiter!

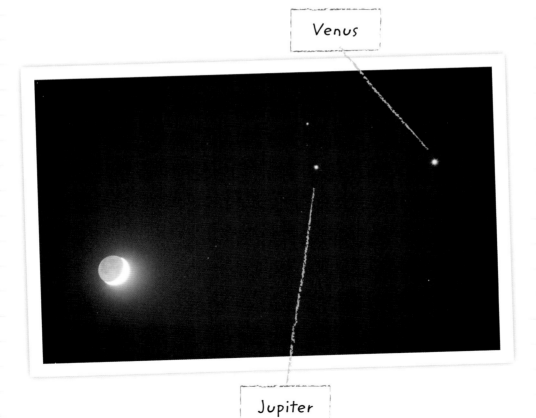

Venus

Jupiter

September 22

While reading yesterday, I found out that some planets can only be seen for a short time in the middle of the night or in the early morning. I don't usually like to wake up early, but I wanted to crawl out of bed to see Mars! Grandpa woke me up at 4:00 a.m. He was still in his pajamas!

Here I am again. I was sleepy, but I really wanted to see Mars.

We grabbed our astronomy kit and walked outside. The sky map showed that Mars would show up in the sky at 4:35 a.m. Right at 4:35 a.m. I began to see a red glow. There it was— Mars!

Now I've seen three planets. Which one will I see next? I can't wait!

Check It Out!

Mars has many volcanoes. They are much bigger than volcanoes on Earth.

October 5

It's exciting to see the planets as they move across the sky, but sometimes it's hard to wait for them. The location of the planets depends on many things. All planets rotate, or spin. Some smaller planets spin faster than the bigger ones. All planets **orbit** around the sun. We can't see them when they're on the part of the path that's on the other side of the sun.

Orbiting Planets

This is my drawing of the planets going around the sun in their orbit paths.

This wasn't true for Jupiter tonight, however. It began to rise 45 minutes after sunset. I looked southwest at Venus and then at the **horizon**, where the sun sets. I had to use binoculars, but I saw Jupiter again. I found the planet by myself! Grandpa would be proud of me!

Jupiter is the largest planet. It is the fifth one from the sun.

13

October 23

Today was my birthday, and Grandpa gave me a telescope! He said that binoculars probably wouldn't be strong enough to help us see the planets Neptune and Uranus because they are so far away. Grandpa wanted me to be able to see them tonight. Actually, I think Grandpa wants to see them as much as I do.

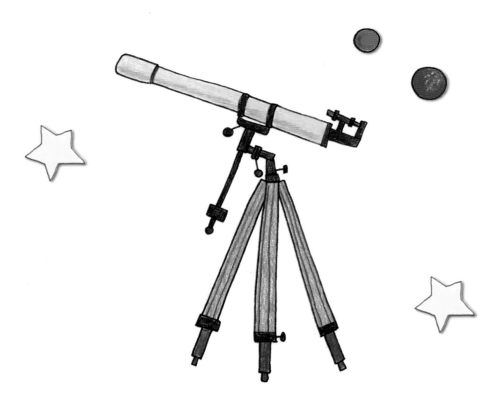

After setting up the telescope and learning how to use it, I looked south. Neptune and Uranus were hard to find, but I could see them. I couldn't see any details, but Neptune looked like a blue dot.

Neptune

Uranus

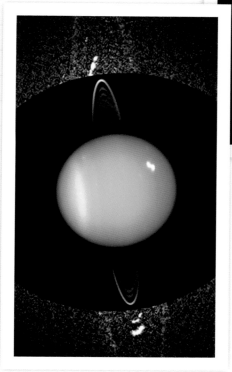

 Check It Out!

- Uranus spins on its side.
- Neptune is the planet that has the fastest winds.

October 24

The sky map said that we could see Saturn at around 4:00 a.m. today, so Grandpa and I got up early. I was excited to try out my telescope again. As I waited, I looked at Mars again. It really is a red planet! The telescope allowed me to see dark, red plains on its surface, and I even saw some white ice caps!

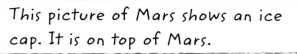

This picture of Mars shows an ice cap. It is on top of Mars.

Finally I saw a creamy-white star that didn't twinkle. It had to be Saturn! Looking through the telescope, I could see a yellow and orange ball that had rings and moons! This telescope is great! Now I can see the colors and parts of the planets just like at the planetarium!

Check It Out!

- Saturn's rings are made of ice chunks and dust.
- It takes Saturn 29 $\frac{1}{2}$ Earth years to go around the sun one time.

Saturn has many rings and moons. It is a beautiful planet.

November 5

The good thing about winter is that it stays dark a long time! This is great for looking at stars. Tonight, Grandpa and I got an early start. We set up the telescope facing southwest before sunset. I hoped I would be able to see Mercury, the closest planet to the sun.

This shows Mercury, Venus, Earth, and Mars just as if they were lined up in a row. It helps you see their sizes next to Earth's size.

Just as the sun fell behind the trees, bright, white Venus appeared. Soon the moon was beside it, and that's when I began looking for Mercury on the horizon. When I did see it, I thought I was looking at the moon because the surface of Mercury has **craters** that looked similar to the ones on the moon. Seeing Mercury means that I have now seen seven planets. I wonder if I'll get to see the last two.

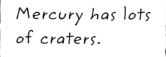

Mercury has lots of craters.

 Check It Out!

Mercury is a very hot planet because it is close to the sun. However, Venus is the hottest planet because clouds cover it and they trap in the sun's heat.

November 12

Mars is so easy to see this month! It is very close to Earth right now because of where it is in its orbit. After looking at the sky map, I know I will be able to look east and see it early this evening. I can't wait!

Most of the land on Mars is like a sandy desert with lots of rocks.

The moon was very bright tonight, so I didn't think Grandpa and I would get a very good view of Mars. We went outside about 6:30 p.m. and it looked like the moon was sitting right on top of Mars. Grandpa and I know about the rovers on Mars. We go to the NASA website almost every day to look at the pictures taken by the rovers. They are amazing!

Two rovers, named Spirit and Opportunity, have been rolling around on Mars, exploring.

December 9

Since I've started looking at the planets, I've never watched them at night and again the next morning. So today Grandpa and I decided that we would see what was in the sky tonight and how it would look early tomorrow morning.

Mars, Venus, and the moon were already shining in the sky when we went outside in the evening. Mars had that red glow and was to the left of the moon and below. We watched for several hours as Mars seemed to follow the moon across the sky.

It would be interesting to see how Mars and the moon move for the rest of the night, but I started to get sleepy. I decided just to look it up on the Internet and draw it in my journal. I need to get up early in the morning!

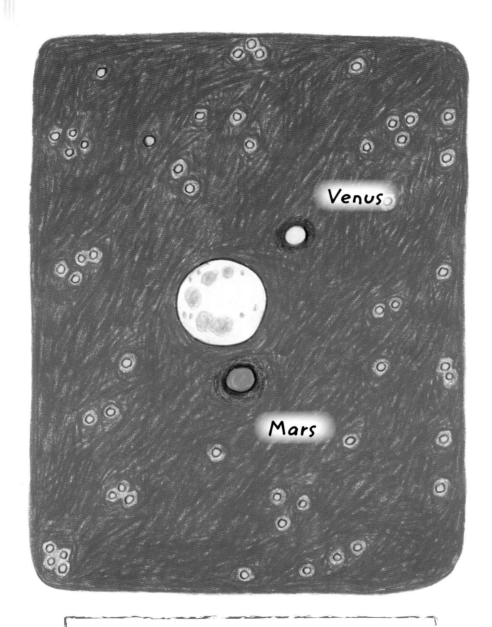

I saw the moon, Mars, and Venus at the same time.

December 10

I was tired all day today! Grandpa and I had only four hours of sleep because we were up so late looking at Mars last night, but it was worth it! When I went outside at 4:00 a.m., I looked southeast. There was Jupiter, close to the horizon. I was excited because I hadn't seen Jupiter with the telescope yet. It was shining more brightly than any of the stars around it.

Check It Out!

The Red Spot on Jupiter is so big that two Earths could fit inside it.

Jupiter's Great Red Spot

I also saw lots of clouds around Jupiter, and one cloud was bigger than the rest. Grandpa said that the cloud is called the *Great Red Spot*. It is actually a huge storm that goes on all the time.

I had no luck finding Mercury today. The light from the rising sun was too bright. I had the sky map. It said that I would find the planet to the left of Jupiter, but I never did see it.

Jupiter

Earth

December 14

In 2006 scientists decided Pluto wasn't a planet. It's really an icy dwarf. Planets all move around the sun on their own paths. Pluto goes around the sun, but Neptune is so much bigger that it can pull Pluto and make it change its path. So now we have 8 planets. That's one less that I'll have to look for, but I'll still miss Pluto.

Planet Distance from the Sun (miles)

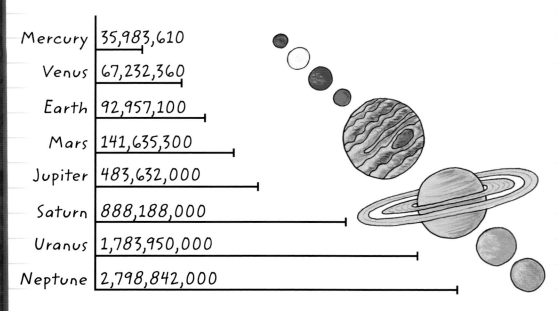

Mercury	35,983,610
Venus	67,232,360
Earth	92,957,100
Mars	141,635,300
Jupiter	483,632,000
Saturn	888,188,000
Uranus	1,783,950,000
Neptune	2,798,842,000

Grandpa thinks I might become an astronomer when I grow up. Then I'll get to watch the planets all the time! Actually, I want to discover new planets, so maybe I will be the person who invents a new space telescope. Now that would be a great job!

So far, I've seen seven planets. I skipped a planet, but I can't figure out which one! I'm too tired to think about it tonight.

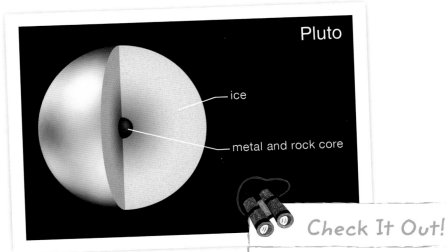

Pluto

ice

metal and rock core

Check It Out!

Pluto is called an icy dwarf instead of a planet because it is made of ice and is much smaller than the planets.

December 31

I realized today which planet I skipped—Earth! I guess I have actually seen eight planets in the last three months. I wish that I lived on another planet so I could look at Earth to see what it looks like and how it moves in space.

I decided to look on the Internet to see if there was a site that would show me what Earth looks like from space. It looks like a big blue ball with some green and brown spots. I can't believe I forgot that Earth is a planet, too! Since I can't travel through space, Earth is the only planet that I can study up close. I've never thought about that before. Maybe I should start another log, all about Earth!

A blanket of air surrounds Earth. It keeps the planet from getting too hot or too cold.

 Check It Out!

Earth is the only planet that has plants and animals—at least that we know about so far!

This is my planet chart. The first time I see a planet, I write the date and the name of the planet. Then I draw a picture. I couldn't decide what date to write for Earth. But then I figured it out—my birthday!

Log

Sept. 3	Venus	
Sept. 7	Jupiter	
Sept. 22	Mars	
Oct. 23	Neptune	
Oct. 23	Uranus	
Oct. 24	Saturn	
Nov. 5	Mercury	
Birth	Earth	

Glossary

astronomy the science of the sun, moon, stars, planets, and other space objects

constellation a group of stars that makes a pattern

crater a large hole in the ground that is shaped like a bowl

horizon the line where the ground and sky meet

orbit to move around an object in a path

planetarium a building with a curved ceiling that uses lights and pictures to show how the sun, moon, stars, and planets move

solar system the moon, stars, planets, and other objects in space that go around the sun

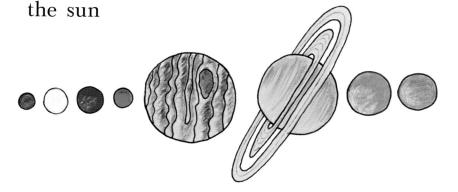

Index

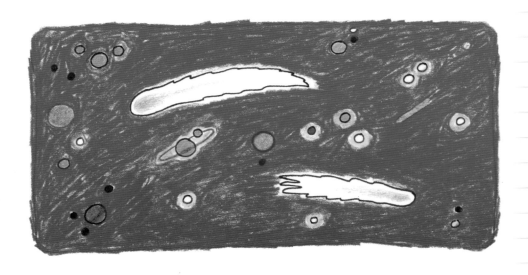